I0500564

Congressional Research Service

State Government Fiscal Stress and Federal Assistance

Robert Jay Dilger
Senior Specialist in American National Government

December 14, 2012

Congressional Research Service

7-5700

www.crs.gov

R41773

Summary

No two state budgets are alike. States have different budget cycles, different ways of preparing revenue estimates and forecasts, different requirements concerning their operating and capital budgets, different roles for their governors in the budget process, and different policies concerning the carrying over of operating budget deficits into the next fiscal year.

Although no two state budgets are alike, all 50 states have experienced fiscal stress in recent years, especially during FY2009 and FY2010. The national economic recession, which officially lasted from December 2007 to June 2009, led to lower levels of economic activity throughout the nation and reduced state tax revenues. State tax revenues from all sources, including sales, personal, and corporate income tax collections, fell from $680.2 billion in FY2008 to $609.8 billion in FY2010, a decline of 10.3%. The decline in state tax revenue, coupled with increased demand for social services and state-balanced operating budget requirements, created what the National Association of State Budget Officers (NASBO) characterized as "one of the worst time periods in state fiscal conditions since the Great Depression."

States closed nearly $230 billion in state budget shortfalls in FY2009 and FY2010; and $146.3 billion in state shortfalls in FY2011 and FY2012. State fiscal conditions improved during FY2011 and FY2012, and are projected to continue to improve in FY2013. However, states continue to experience fiscal challenges. For example, although state general fund revenue is projected to surpass pre-recession levels in FY2013 by about $13 billion (from $680.2 billion in FY2008 to $692.8 billion in FY2013), total general fund spending is projected to remain below pre-recession levels in FY2013 (from $687.3 billion in FY2008 to $681.3 billion in FY2013). State budget officers predict continuing budgetary challenges in virtually all states in FY2013, in part due to slow state revenue growth, the withdrawal of temporary federal assistance provided through P.L. 111-5, the American Recovery and Reinvestment Act of 2009 (ARRA), the need to replenish reserves, and increased costs for health care and other social services.

Congressional interest in state budgetary finances has increased in recent years, primarily because state action to address budget shortfalls, such as increasing taxes, laying off or furloughing state employees, and postponing or eliminating state infrastructure projects, could have an adverse effect on the national economic recovery. For example, Federal Reserve Board Chairman Benjamin Bernanke stated on March 2, 2011, that the fiscal problems of state and local governments have "had national implications, as their spending cuts and tax increases have been a headwind on the economic recovery." Also, if states reduce their service levels there could be additional pressure for the federal government to provide those services. As funding from ARRA expires, there could be additional pressure for the federal government to provide additional federal assistance to states.

This report examines the current status of state fiscal conditions and the role of federal assistance in state budgets. It begins with a brief overview of state budgeting procedures and then provides budgetary data comparing state fiscal conditions in FY2008 to FY2011. The data indicate that (1) states reduced their general fund budgets from FY2008 to FY2011, but, because they received increased federal funding, increased their total amount of spending; (2) the share of total state expenditures held by the states' four operating expenditures budgets (general fund, federal funds, other state funds, and bonds) shifted from FY2008 to FY2011, with an increased reliance on federal funds; and (3) states experienced varying levels of fiscal stress from FY2008 to FY2011.

This report concludes with an assessment of the consequences current levels of state fiscal stress may have for the 113th Congress.

Contents

Figures

Tables

Contacts

State Budgets

No two state budgets are alike.[1] For example, 27 states have an annual budget cycle, 21 states have a biennial budget cycle, and 2 states have an annual budget cycle for some agencies or purposes and a biennial budget cycle for others.[2] Most states (46) begin their fiscal year on July 1, 2 states begin their fiscal year on October 1 (Alabama and Michigan), 1 state begins its fiscal year on September 1 (Texas), and 1 state begins its fiscal year on April 1 (New York).[3]

States also have different ways of preparing their revenue estimates and forecasts that project the amount of revenue that will be available based on current law to support operating costs and capital outlays in the current and future fiscal years. These revenue estimates are important because they establish the general parameters for the state's budget at the outset of the budget process.[4] The state budget office is solely responsible for revenue forecasting in 13 states, a board or commission is solely responsible in 11 states, and the state revenue office is solely responsible in 3 states. The remaining states use a combination of agencies or boards to develop their revenue forecasts.[5]

All but one state (Vermont) has some form of a balanced operating budget requirement, either in statute or in their state constitution, but the stringency of these requirements varies, ranging from having only a requirement that the governor submit a balanced operating budget for the legislature's consideration (2 states) to having a prohibition against carrying a deficit forward and requirements that the governor propose, the legislature pass, and the governor sign a balanced operating budget (26 states).[6] Overall, governors in 44 states must submit a balanced operating budget for legislative consideration, state legislatures in 41 states must pass a balanced operating

---

[1] The state expenditure data presented in this report are drawn from the National Association of State Budget Officers' (NASBO) annual State Expenditure Reports. The data are self-reported by the states. In 2010, the Government Accountability Office (GAO) assessed the reliability of NASBO expenditure data for a report on state and local government use of funding provided by P.L. 111-5, the American Recovery and Reinvestment Act of 2009. GAO reviewed existing documentation related to the NASBO data sources and interviewed knowledgeable agency officials about the data. GAO determined that "the data are sufficiently reliable for the purposes of this report." See U.S. Government Accountability Office, *Recovery Act: Opportunities to Improve Management and Strengthen Accountability over States' and Localities' Use of Funds*, GAO-10-999, September 20, 2010, p. 205, at http://www.gao.gov/new.items/d10999.pdf. GAO has also examined the reliability of NASBO's semi-annual Fiscal Survey of States reports and found them to be reliable. See U.S. Government Accountability Office, *State and Local Governments: Knowledge of Past Recessions Can Inform Future Federal Assistance*, GAO-11-401, March 31, 2011, pp. 2, 52, at http://www.gao.gov/new.items/d11401.pdf. The Bureau of the Census also surveys state and local governments concerning their revenues and expenditures. NASBO data was used in this report because it includes more recent estimates.

[2] National Association of State Budget Officers, *Budget Processes in the States*, Washington, DC, Summer 2008, p. 5, at http://nasbo.org/LinkClick.aspx?fileticket=AaAKTnjgucg%3d&tabid=38.

[3] Ibid.

[4] Ibid., pp. 3, 20. For further information and analysis of state revenue estimates see Susan K. Urahn and Thomas Gais, "States' Revenue Estimating: Cracks in the Crystal Ball," The Nelson Rockefeller Institute of Government and the Pew Center on the States, Washington, DC, at http://www.pewcenteronthestates.org/uploadedFiles/States_Revenue_Estimating_final.pdf.

[5] National Association of State Budget Officers, *Budget Processes in the States*, Washington, DC, Summer 2008, pp. 3, 20, at http://nasbo.org/LinkClick.aspx?fileticket=AaAKTnjgucg%3d&tabid=38.Ibid.

[6] Ibid., p. 40; and National Conference of State Legislatures, "NCSL Fiscal Brief: State Balanced Budget Provisions," Washington, DC, October 2010, pp. 4, 5, at http://www.ncsl.org/documents/fiscal/StateBalancedBudgetProvisions2010.pdf.

---

budget, the governor must sign a balanced operating budget in 37 states, and 43 states have a prohibition against carrying an operating budget deficit forward.[7] Also, the extent of the governor's authority in the budget process varies among the states. The governor can spend unanticipated federal funds in 30 states, reduce enacted budgets in 38 states, veto an item within the appropriations bill in 41 states, veto selected words in 15 states, and use the veto to change the meaning of words in 4 states.[8]

Although 43 states have a prohibition against carrying an operating budget deficit forward, all states incur debt to finance capital projects, typically subject to limits on debt service (31 states), levels of authorized debt (44 states), or both (29 states).[9] State government long-term debt was $1.098 trillion at the end of FY2010 (39.2% of total state and local government debt), an increase of 5.8% from FY2009.[10]

Although no two state budgets are alike, all 50 states experienced heightened levels of fiscal stress during FY2009 and FY2010.[11] The national economic recession, which officially lasted from December 2007 to June 2009, led to lower levels of economic activity throughout the nation and reduced state tax revenues.

State tax revenues from all sources, including sales, personal, and corporate income tax collections, fell from $680.2 billion in FY2008 to $609.8 billion in FY2010, a decline of 10.3%.[12] The decline in state tax revenue, coupled with state balanced operating budget requirements, created what the National Association of State Budget Officers (NASBO) characterized as "one of the worst time periods in state fiscal conditions since the Great Depression."[13] For example, even with an additional $120.3 billion in temporary federal assistance provided through P.L. 111-5, the American Recovery and Reinvestment Act of 2009 (ARRA), in FY2010, states reduced their general fund expenditures by 5.7% from FY2009 ($660.9 billion) to FY2010 ($623.4 billion), enacted $23.9 billion in increased taxes and fees, and raised an additional $7.5 billion through other revenue measures.[14]

States closed nearly $230 billion in state budget shortfalls in FY2009 and FY2010; and $146.3 billion in FY2011 and FY2012.[15] State fiscal conditions improved somewhat in FY2011 and

---

[7] National Association of State Budget Officers, *Budget Processes in the States*, Washington, DC, Summer 2008, pp. 29, 40, at http://nasbo.org/LinkClick.aspx?fileticket=AaAKTnjgucg%3d&tabid=38.

[8] Ibid., pp. 29, 38.

[9] Ibid., p. 43.

[10] U.S. Census Bureau, *State Government Finances Summary: 2010*, Government Division Briefs, January 2012, p. 2, at http://www2.census.gov/govs/state/10statesummaryreport.pdf. For further analysis of state debt issues see CRS Report R41735, *State and Local Government Debt: An Analysis*, by Steven Maguire.

[11] National Association of State Budget Officers, *The Fiscal Survey of States*, Washington, DC, fall 2010, pp. vii, viii, at http://nasbo.org/LinkClick.aspx?fileticket=C6q1M3kxaEY%3d&tabid=83.

[12] National Association of State Budget Officers, *The Fiscal Survey of States*, Washington, DC, fall 2011, pp. 4-6, at http://nasbo.org/LinkClick.aspx?fileticket=y%2fqdEfOcPfs%3d&tabid=38.

[13] National Association of State Budget Officers, *The Fiscal Survey of States*, Washington, DC, fall 2010, p. vii, at http://nasbo.org/LinkClick.aspx?fileticket=C6q1M3kxaEY%3d&tabid=83.

[14] Ibid., pp. vii, viii; National Association of State Budget Officers, *The Fiscal Survey of States*, Washington, DC, Fall 2011, p. 4, at http://nasbo.org/LinkClick.aspx?fileticket=y%2fqdEfOcPfs%3d&tabid=38; and National Association of State Budget Officers, *State Expenditure Report: Fiscal Year 2010*, Washington, DC, December 2011, p. 2, at http://nasbo.org/LinkClick.aspx?fileticket=5VMZ59stp1w%3d&tabid=38.

[15] National Association of State Budget Officers, *The Fiscal Survey of States*, Washington, DC, spring 2011, p. i, http://nasbo.org/LinkClick.aspx?fileticket=yNV8Jv3X7Is%3d&tabid=65; and National Association of State Budget (continued...)

FY2012, and are projected to continue to improve in FY2013. However, states continue to experience fiscal challenges. For example, although state general fund revenue is projected to surpass pre-recession levels in FY2013 by about $13 billion (from $680.2 billion in FY2008 to $692.8 billion in FY2013), total general fund spending is projected to remain below pre-recession levels in FY2013 (from $687.3 billion in FY2008 to $681.3 billion in FY2013).[16] State budget officers predict continuing budgetary challenges in virtually all states in FY2013, in part due to slow state revenue growth, the withdrawal of temporary federal assistance provided through P.L. 111-5, the American Recovery and Reinvestment Act of 2009 (ARRA), the need to replenish reserves, and increased costs for health care and other social services. In addition, projected costs for state employee pension and retirement health care obligations and delayed infrastructure projects are also expected to provide continuing budgetary challenges for states.[17]

Congressional interest in state budgetary finances has increased in recent years, primarily because state action to address budget shortfalls, such as increasing taxes, laying off or furloughing state employees, and postponing or eliminating state infrastructure projects, could have an adverse effect on the national economic recovery. For example, Federal Reserve Board Chairman Benjamin Bernanke stated on March 2, 2011, that the fiscal problems of state and local governments have "had national implications, as their spending cuts and tax increases have been a headwind on the economic recovery."[18] He also stated, on November 20, 2012, that "state and local governments have cut about 600,000 jobs on net since the third quarter of 2008 while reducing real expenditures for infrastructure projects by 20 percent."[19] In addition, as funding from ARRA expires, there could be additional pressure for the federal government to provide additional federal assistance to states.

This report examines the current status of state fiscal conditions and the role of federal assistance in state budgets. It begins with a brief overview of state budgeting procedures and then provides budgetary data comparing state fiscal conditions in FY2008 to FY2011. As will be discussed, the data presented in this report indicate that (1) states reduced their general fund budgets from FY2008 to FY2011, but, because they received increased federal funding, increased their total amount of spending; (2) the share of total state expenditures held by the states' four operating

---

(...continued)

Officers, *The Fiscal Survey of States*, Washington, DC, Spring 2012, p. vii, at http://www.nasbo.org/publications-data/fiscal-survey-of-the-states.

[16] National Association of State Budget Officers, *The Fiscal Survey of States*, Washington, DC, fall 2012, p. viii, at http://www.nasbo.org/publications-data/fiscal-survey-of-the-states.

[17] National Association of State Budget Officers, "Facts You Should Know: State and Local Bankruptcy, Municipal Bonds, State and Local Pensions," Washington, DC, 2010, at http://www.nasbo.org/LinkClick.aspx?fileticket= TPVfxV3%2fn10%3d&tabid=38; Dean Baker, "The Origins and Severity of the Public Pension Crisis," Center for Economic and Policy Research, Washington, DC, February 2011, at http://www.cepr.net/documents/publications/pensions-2011-02.pdf; The Pew Center on the States, "The Trillion Dollar Gap: Underfunded State Retirement Systems and the Road Ahead," Washington, DC, February 2010, at http://downloads.pewcenteronthestates.org/The_Trillion_Dollar_Gap_final.pdf; The Pew Center on the States, "The Widening Gap Update," Washington, DC, June 18, 2012, at http://www.pewstates.org/uploadedFiles/PCS_Assets/2012/Pew_Pensions_Update.pdf; and CRS Report R41736, *State and Local Pension Plans and Fiscal Distress: A Legal Overview*, by Jennifer Staman.

[18] Benjamin S. Bernanke, Chairman, Board of Governors of the Federal Reserve Board, "Challenges for State and Local Governments," presentation at the 2011 Annual Awards Dinner of the Citizens Budget Commission, New York, March 2, 2011, at http://www.federalreserve.gov/newsevents/speech/bernanke20110302a.htm.

[19] Benjamin S. Bernanke, Chairman, Board of Governors of the Federal Reserve Board, "The Economic Recovery and Economic Policy," presentation at the New York Economic Club, New York, November 20, 2012, at http://www.federalreserve.gov/newsevents/speech/bernanke20121120a.htm.

---

expenditures budgets (general fund, federal funds, other state funds, and bonds) shifted from FY2008 to FY2011, with an increased reliance on federal funds; and (3) states experienced varying levels of fiscal stress from FY2008 to FY2011. This report concludes with an assessment of the consequences current levels of state fiscal stress may have for the 113th Congress.

State Budgetary Procedures

Unlike the federal government, states budget separately for current operating expenditures and for capital expenditures. As mentioned previously, virtually all states (except Vermont) have some form of a balanced operating budget requirement, and most states have restrictions on the amount of debt that they issue to finance capital projects.[20]

Current State Operating Expenditures

Most states account for their current operating expenditures through four budgets:

- the *state general fund budget* refers to expenditures from revenues accruing to the state from taxes, fees, interest earnings, and other sources which can be used for the general operation of state government.

- the *state federal funds budget* refers to expenditures from funds received directly from the federal government.

- the *other state funds budget* refers to expenditures from revenue sources that are restricted by law for particular governmental functions or activities; for example, a gasoline tax dedicated to a state highway trust fund would appear in other state funds.

- the *state bonds budget* refers to expenditures from the sale of bonds, generally for capital projects.[21]

Also, 48 states (Kansas and Montana are the exceptions) have a state budget stabilization fund, budget reserve account, or "rainy day" fund to cover unanticipated revenue shortfalls.[22] The amount of revenue set aside in these funds varies from state-to-state, generally ranging from 3% to 10% of appropriations.[23] Most budget analysts suggest as an informal rule-of-thumb that states set aside at least 5% of expenditures for unanticipated budget shortfalls.[24]

---

[20] National Association of State Budget Officers, *Budget Processes in the States*, Washington, DC, summer 2008, pp. 40, 43, at http://nasbo.org/LinkClick.aspx?fileticket=AaAKTnjgucg%3d&tabid=38.

[21] Ibid., p. 107; and National Association of State Budget Officers, *State Expenditure Report: Fiscal Year 2009*, Washington, DC, December 2010, p. 4, at http://www.nasbo.org/LinkClick.aspx?fileticket=w7RqO74llEw%3d&tabid=79.

[22] National Association of State Budget Officers, *Budget Processes in the States*, Washington, DC, summer 2008, pp. 67-69, at http://nasbo.org/LinkClick.aspx?fileticket=AaAKTnjgucg%3d&tabid=38.

[23] National Association of State Budget Officers, *The Fiscal Survey of States*, Washington, DC, fall 2012, p. 51, at http://www.nasbo.org/publications-data/fiscal-survey-of-the-states. The procedures used to expend these funds vary from state-to-state, with some states requiring a majority vote of the state legislature and others requiring a super majority vote to access the funds. See National Association of State Budget Officers, *Budget Processes in the States*, Washington, DC, summer 2008, p. 50, at http://nasbo.org/LinkClick.aspx?fileticket=AaAKTnjgucg%3d&tabid=38.

[24] National Association of State Budget Officers, *The Fiscal Survey of States*, Washington, DC, fall 2012, p. 51, at (continued...)

State end-of-year balances, which include ending balances and budget stabilization, budget reserve account, and "rainy day" funds, declined from 8.6% of total state expenditures in FY2008 ($59.1 billion) to 5.2% in FY2010 ($32.5 billion). Since then, states have increased their budget reserves, with state end-of-year balances projected to reach 9.0% of total state expenditures in FY2013 ($61.3 billion).[25] However, state budget officials note that the combined balances for Texas and Alaska ($12.7 billion and $17.1 billion, respectively) account for $48.5% of total state end-of-year balances. The remaining 48 states have average projected end-of-year balances of 5.0% of total state expenditures, with 5 states projecting end-of-year balances below 1% of total state expenditures and 19 others projecting end-of-year balances greater than 1% of total state expenditures, but less than the recommended 5% level.[26]

The State Capital Budget

The state capital budget is associated with the acquisition or construction of major capital projects, including land, buildings, structures, and major equipment. Minor repairs and routine maintenance are typically reported as operating expenses. Funds for capital projects traditionally have come primarily from non-general fund sources. In FY2010, funds for capital projects came from bonds (37.6%), dedicated fees and surpluses (30.8%), federal funds (26.8% in FY2009), and state general funds/end-of-year operating surpluses (4.8% in FY2009).[27]

State capital spending totaled $80.3 billion in FY2008, $84.2 billion in FY2009, $86.1 billion in FY2010, and an estimated $86.1 billion in FY2011.[28] According to NASBO, the increase in state capital spending in FY2009 and FY2010 was at least partly due to increased federal funding provided by ARRA and several ARRA bond provisions, such as Build America Bonds, Recovery Zone Economic Development Bonds, and School Construction Bonds.[29] In FY2010, transportation projects accounted for 57.0% ($49.1 billion) of all state capital expenditures, followed by higher education projects at 14.3% ($12.3 billion), environmental projects at 5.9% ($5.1 billion), corrections projects at 1.8% ($1.6 billion), housing projects at 1.5% ($1.3 billion) and other capital projects, such as public school facilities, zoo improvements, health care infrastructure, and sports facilities, at 19.5% ($16.7 billion).[30]

(...continued)

http://www.nasbo.org/publications-data/fiscal-survey-of-the-states.

[25] Ibid.

[26] Ibid.

[27] National Association of State Budget Officers, *State Expenditure Report: Fiscal Year 2010*, Washington, DC, December 2011, p. 78, at http://nasbo.org/LinkClick.aspx?fileticket=5VMZ59stp1w%3d&tabid=38.

[28] National Association of State Budget Officers, *State Expenditure Report: Fiscal Year 2009*, Washington, DC, December 2010, p. 80, at http://www.nasbo.org/LinkClick.aspx?fileticket=w7RqO74llEw%3d&tabid=79; and National Association of State Budget Officers, *State Expenditure Report: Fiscal Year 2010*, Washington, DC, December 2011, p. 78, at http://nasbo.org/LinkClick.aspx?fileticket=5VMZ59stp1w%3d&tabid=38.

[29] For further analysis of Build America Bonds, Recovery Zone Economic Development Bonds, and School Construction Bonds, see CRS Report R40523, *Tax Credit Bonds: Overview and Analysis*, by Steven Maguire.

[30] National Association of State Budget Officers, *State Expenditure Report: Fiscal Year 2010*, Washington, DC, December 2011, p. 79, at http://nasbo.org/LinkClick.aspx?fileticket=5VMZ59stp1w%3d&tabid=38.

Trends in State Expenditures

This section examines trends in state expenditures, in nominal dollars, from FY2008 to FY2011, starting with total state expenditures (including the states' capital budgets) and followed by each of the states' four operating expenditures budgets (state general fund, federal funds, other state funds, and bonds). FY2008 is used as the starting point for comparative purposes in most of the discussion because FY2008 is used by many in Congress as the baseline for making comparisons in federal budget debates.[31]

Three general conclusions can be drawn from the data presented in the following tables. First, states reduced their general fund budgets from FY2008 to FY2011, but increased their total amount of spending. Faced with declining own-source revenue, states reduced their general fund budgets by $51.6 billion from FY2008 to FY2011 (from $687.9 billion in FY2008 to an estimated $636.3 billion in FY2011). However, because expenditures from the states' federal funds budgets increased by $186.6 billion from FY2008 to FY2011 (from $388.2 billion in FY2008 to an estimated $574.8 billion in FY2011), expenditures from other state funds budgets increased $57.7 billion from FY2008 to FY2011 (from $376.9 billion in FY2008 to $434.6 billion in FY2011) and expenditures from state bonds budgets increased by $6.7 billion (from $34.8 billion in FY2008 to $41.5 billion in FY2011), total state expenditures increased by $208.3 billion from FY2008 to FY2011 (from nearly $1.5 trillion in FY2008 to nearly $1.7 trillion in FY2011). Media reports of state budget cuts and reports of the need for states to make future budget cuts typically refer to the states' general fund budgets or to budget cuts necessary to maintain current service levels, not to total state expenditures. The possible implications of the projected decrease in state federal assistance over the next several years, for both Congress and the states, are discussed later in this report.

Second, as shown in **Figure 1**, the share of total state expenditures held by the states' four operating expenditures budgets shifted from FY2008 to FY2011, with an increased reliance on federal funds. For example, in FY2008, the states' general fund budgets accounted for 45.9% of total state spending, their federal funds budgets accounted for 26.3%, their other state funds budgets accounted for 25.5%, and their bonds budgets accounted for 2.3%. In FY2011, the states' general fund budgets accounted for an estimated 37.7% of total state spending, their federal funds budgets accounted for an estimated 34.1%, their other state funds budgets accounted for an estimated 25.4%, and their bonds budgets accounted for an estimated 2.3%.[32] The possible implications for Congress, and for the states, of the states' increased reliance on federal funds are discussed later in this report.

Third, the data suggest that states experienced varying levels of fiscal stress from FY2008 to FY2011. For example, if state fiscal stress had been evenly distributed, the change in total state expenditures and the change in state general fund expenditures from FY2008 to FY2011 would have been expected to be fairly evenly distributed across states. However, the change in total state expenditures varied across the states, ranging from a reduction of $3.725 billion in Connecticut to an increase of $33.077 billion in California. Overall, from FY2008 to FY2011, 5 states reduced

---

[31] For example, H.Res. 38, Reducing non-security spending to fiscal year 2008 levels or less, was passed by the House of Representatives, by a vote of 256-165, on January 25, 2011.

[32] National Association of State Budget Officers, *State Expenditure Report: Fiscal Year 2010*, Washington, DC, December 2011, p. 5, at http://nasbo.org/LinkClick.aspx?fileticket=5VMZ59stp1w%3d&tabid=38.

their total expenditures and 45 increased their total expenditures. Also, the change in state general fund expenditures also varied across the states, ranging from a reduction of $11.5 billion in California to an increase of $3.7 billion in Alaska. Overall, from FY2008 to FY2011, 11 states increased their general fund expenditures and 39 states cut their general fund expenditures.

The variation in state fiscal stress experienced from FY2008 to FY2011 is typical of state responses to past national economic downturns. As the Government Accountability Office (GAO) has reported, "revenue fluctuations during national recessions vary substantially across states ... due in part to states' differing tax structures, economic conditions, and industrial bases."[33] Also, unemployment rates have varied across states during both the most recent and past recessions and GAO has found that "while economic downturns within states generally occur around the same time as national recessions, their timing—or entrance into and exit out of the economic downturn—and duration varies."[34] The implications for Congress of these variations in state fiscal stress, as well as various ways to measure state fiscal stress, are discussed later in this report.

---

[33] U.S. Government Accountability Office, *State and Local Governments: Knowledge of Past Recessions Can Inform Future Federal Fiscal Assistance*, GAO-11-401, March 31, 2010, p. 15, at http://www.gao.gov/new.items/d11401.pdf.

[34] Ibid., p. 6.

Figure 1. Total State Expenditures for FY2000-FY2011, by Funding Source

(% of total state expenditures)

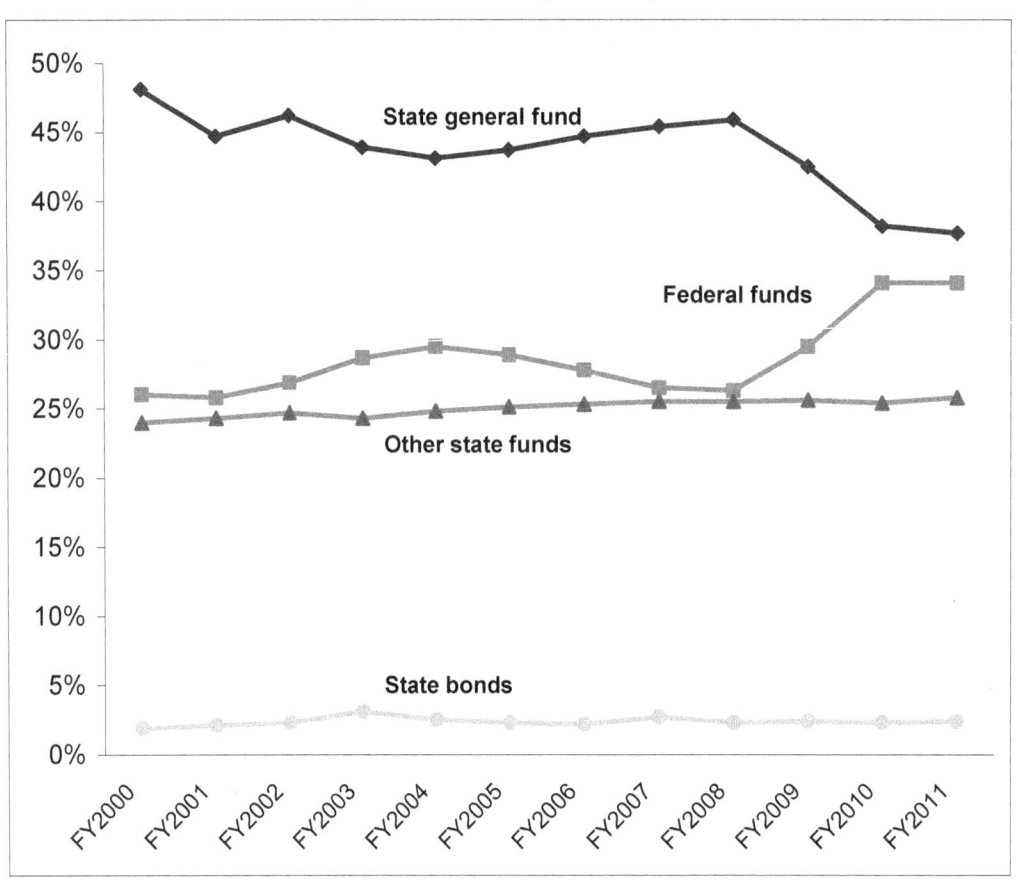

Source: National Association of State Budget Officers, *State Expenditure Report [FYs 2000-2009]*, Washington, DC, all p. 2, at http://www.nasbo.org/Publications/StateExpenditureReport/StateExpenditureReportArchives/ tabid/107/Default.aspx; and National Association of State Budget Officers, *FY2010 State Expenditure Report*, Washington, DC, December 2011, p. 7, at http://nasbo.org/LinkClick.aspx?fileticket=5VMZ59stp1w%3d&tabid= 38.

Note: FY2011 total state expenditures and share from the state general fund, federal funds, other state funds, and state bonds are estimated from state budget documents.

Total State Expenditures

As shown in **Table 1**, total state expenditures (capital inclusive) increased every fiscal year from FY2000 through FY2011, ranging from an increase of $39,054 million in FY2003 to $85,066 million in FY2005. In percentage terms, total state expenditures increased, on average, by 5.4% from FY2000 to FY2011, ranging from an increase of 3.59% in FY2003 to an increase of 7.48% in FY2000. In recent years, total state expenditures have increased more slowly than in the past— 3.77% in FY2008, 5.38% in FY2009, 4.04% in FY2010, and an estimated 4.05% in FY2011.

Table 1. Total State Expenditures (Capital Inclusive), FY2000-FY2011

($ in millions)

FY	Total Amount of State Expenditures	Change in Total Amount of State Expenditures from Previous FY	% Change in Total Amount of State Expenditures from Previous FY
2000	$946,086	$65,834	7.48%
2001	$1,015,813	$69,727	7.37%
2002	$1,088,207	$72,394	7.13%
2003	$1,127,261	$39,054	3.59%
2004	$1,181,330	$54,069	4.80%
2005	$1,266,396	$85,066	7.20%
2006	$1,343,118	$76,722	6.06%
2007	$1,425,028	$81,910	6.10%
2008	$1,478,782	$53,754	3.77%
2009	$1,558,416	$79,634	5.38%
2010	$1,621,370	$62,954	4.04%
2011 est.	$1,687,096	$65,726	4.05%

Source: National Association of State Budget Officers, *State Expenditure Report [FYs 2000-2009]*, Washington, DC, all p. 2, at http://www.nasbo.org/Publications/StateExpenditureReport/StateExpenditureReportArchives/tabid/107/Default.aspx; and National Association of State Budget Officers, *State Expenditure Report: FY2010*, Washington, DC, December 2011, p. 7, at http://nasbo.org/LinkClick.aspx?fileticket=5VMZ59stp1w%3d&tabid=38.

As shown in **Table 2**, total state expenditures (capital inclusive) increased by more than $208.3 billion from FY2008 to FY2011 (from $1,478,782 million in FY2008 to $1,687,096 million in FY2011). Five states (Connecticut, Delaware, Nevada, New Jersey, and Vermont) decreased their total amount of state expenditures and 45 states increased their total amount of state expenditures.

Table 2. Change in Total State Expenditures, FY2008-FY2011

($ in millions)

State	Total State Expenditures, FY2008	Total State Expenditures, FY2011	Change in Total State Expenditures, FY2008 to FY2011
Alabama	$19,840	$20,843	$1,003
Alaska	$11,656	$13,923	$2,267
Arizona	$25,247	$29,264	$4,017
Arkansas	$16,899	$20,333	$3,434
California	$194,276	$227,353	$33,077
Colorado	$25,129	$28,462	$3,333
Connecticut	$24,270	$20,545	($3,725)
Delaware	$8,621	$8,412	($209)

State	Total State Expenditures, FY2008	Total State Expenditures, FY2011	Change in Total State Expenditures, FY2008 to FY2011
Florida	$64,379	$70,518	$6,139
Georgia	$38,494	$39,166	$672
Hawaii	$11,160	$11,222	$62
Idaho	$5,932	$7,050	$1,118
Illinois	$44,566	$56,222	$11,656
Indiana	$24,239	$27,042	$2,803
Iowa	$16,129	$18,538	$2,409
Kansas	$12,689	$14,778	$2,089
Kentucky	$22,995	$25,528	$2,533
Louisiana	$28,888	$30,174	$1,286
Maine	$7,427	$8,171	$744
Maryland	$30,408	$34,795	$4,387
Massachusetts	$43,807	$51,761	$7,954
Michigan	$43,982	$50,020	$6,038
Minnesota	$28,446	$32,082	$3,636
Mississippi	$15,539	$19,777	$4,238
Missouri	$21,432	$24,728	$3,296
Montana	$5,357	$6,164	$807
Nebraska	$8,711	$9,802	$1,091
Nevada	$9,240	$8,549	($691)
New Hampshire	$4,807	$5,435	$628
New Jersey	$48,704	$48,235	($469)
New Mexico	$14,207	$14,829	$622
New York	$116,056	$132,765	$16,709
North Carolina	$41,588	$51,124	$9,536
North Dakota	$3,597	$4,974	$1,377
Ohio	$56,763	$60,314	$3,551
Oklahoma	$20,730	$22,067	$1,337
Oregon	$22,174	$33,455	$11,281
Pennsylvania	$58,696	$70,089	$11,393
Rhode Island	$7,118	$8,292	$1,174
South Carolina	$20,787	$25,691	$4,904
South Dakota	$3,217	$3,781	$564
Tennessee	$26,033	$30,904	$4,871
Texas	$81,097	$94,443	$13,346

State	Total State Expenditures, FY2008	Total State Expenditures, FY2011	Change in Total State Expenditures, FY2008 to FY2011
Utah	$11,323	$13,372	$2,049
Vermont	$5,308	$4,827	($481)
Virginia	$35,330	$42,470	$7,140
Washington	$31,732	$32,430	$698
West Virginia	$18,710	$21,492	$2,782
Wisconsin	$36,089	$42,844	$6,755
Wyoming	$4,958	$8,041	$3,083
Total	$1,478,782	$1,687,096	$208,314

Source: CRS computations from National Association of State Budget Officers, *State Expenditure Report: FY2009*, Washington, DC, p. 6, at http://nasbo.org/LinkClick.aspx?fileticket=%2bPqnl4oZw2l%3d&tabid=79 and National Association of State Budget Officers, *State Expenditure Report: FY2010*, Washington, DC, December 2011, p. 7, at http://nasbo.org/LinkClick.aspx?fileticket=5VMZ59stp1w%3d&tabid=38.

Notes: Total state expenditures include expenditures from the state's general fund account, federal funds account, other state funds, and bonds. FY2011 total state expenditures are estimated from state budget documents.

State General Fund Expenditures

In contrast to total state expenditures, which increased by $208.3 billion from FY2008 to FY2011, state general fund expenditures decreased by nearly $42.7 billion from FY2008 ($678.9 billion) to FY2011 ($636.3 billion). As shown in **Table 3**, from FY2008 to FY2011, 39 states decreased their state general fund expenditures and 11 states (Alaska, Arkansas, Illinois, Indiana, Nebraska, North Dakota, Ohio, Virginia, Washington, Wisconsin, and Wyoming) increased their state general fund expenditures.

Table 3. Change in State General Fund Expenditures, FY2008-FY2011

($ in millions)

State	State General Fund Expenditures, FY2008	State General Fund Expenditures, FY2011	Change in State General Fund Expenditures, FY2008 to FY2011
Alabama	$8,460	$6,507	($1,953)
Alaska	$5,090	$8,878	$3,788
Arizona	$10,368	$8,676	($1,692)
Arkansas	$4,274	$4,442	$168
California	$102,986	$91,480	($11,506)
Colorado	$7,908	$6,984	($924)
Connecticut	$16,627	$11,969	($4,658)
Delaware	$3,422	$3,271	($151)
Florida	$27,513	$24,046	($3,467)

State	State General Fund Expenditures, FY2008	State General Fund Expenditures, FY2011	Change in State General Fund Expenditures, FY2008 to FY2011
Georgia	$17,934	$15,954	($1,980)
Hawaii	$5,407	$4,969	($438)
Idaho	$2,799	$2,388	($411)
Illinois	$22,140	$22,902	$762
Indiana	$12,880	$13,037	$157
Iowa	$5,867	$5,348	($519)
Kansas	$6,102	$5,727	($375)
Kentucky	$9,334	$8,787	($547)
Louisiana	$10,372	$7,951	($2,421)
Maine	$3,084	$2,858	($226)
Maryland	$14,488	$13,262	($1,226)
Massachusetts	$28,934	$28,468	($466)
Michigan	$9,822	$8,386	($1,436)
Minnesota	$17,600	$16,478	($1,122)
Mississippi	$4,842	$4,344	($498)
Missouri	$8,084	$7,616	($468)
Montana	$1,901	$1,701	($200)
Nebraska	$3,247	$3,322	$75
Nevada	$4,031	$3,401	($630)
New Hampshire	$1,515	$1,322	($193)
New Jersey	$33,112	$29,322	($3,790)
New Mexico	$6,027	$5,203	($824)
New York	$53,385	$53,313	($72)
North Carolina	$20,376	$18,503	($1,873)
North Dakota	$1,204	$1,585	$381
Ohio	$25,722	$27,649	$1,927
Oklahoma	$6,793	$6,475	($318)
Oregon	$6,601	$6,107	($494)
Pennsylvania	$26,969	$25,142	($1,827)
Rhode Island	$3,405	$2,974	($431)
South Carolina	$7,149	$5,080	($2,069)
South Dakota	$1,176	$1,148	($28)
Tennessee	$11,570	$11,227	($343)
Texas	$41,184	$40,541	($643)
Utah	$5,784	$4,710	($1,074)

State	State General Fund Expenditures, FY2008	State General Fund Expenditures, FY2011	Change in State General Fund Expenditures, FY2008 to FY2011
Vermont	$1,225	$822	($403)
Virginia	$15,099	$16,435	$1,336
Washington	$14,616	$14,825	$209
West Virginia	$3,824	$3,793	($31)
Wisconsin	$13,527	$13,565	$38
Wyoming	$3,132	$3,364	$232
Total	$678,911	$636,257	($42,654)

Source: CRS computations from National Association of State Budget Officers, *State Expenditure Report: FY2009*, Washington, DC, p. 6, at http://nasbo.org/LinkClick.aspx?fileticket=%2bPqnl4oZw2I%3d&tabid=79 and National Association of State Budget Officers, *State Expenditure Report: FY2010*, Washington, DC, December 2011, p. 7, at http://nasbo.org/LinkClick.aspx?fileticket=5VMZ59stp1w%3d&tabid=38.

Notes: FY2011 state general fund expenditures are estimated from state budget documents.

State Federal Funds Expenditures

As mentioned previously, most of the increase in total state expenditures from FY2008 to FY2011 came from the states' federal funds expenditures budgets. States spent $388.2 billion in federal assistance in FY2008, $463.0 billion in FY2009, $552.7 billion in FY2010, and an estimated $574.8 billion in FY2011.

As shown in **Table 4**, state federal funds expenditures increased nearly $186.6 billion from FY2008 to FY2011. One state (Louisiana) decreased its federal funds expenditures and 49 states increased their federal funds expenditures.

Table 4. Change in State Federal Funds Expenditures, FY2008-FY2011

($ in millions)

State	State Federal Funds Expenditures, FY2008	State Federal Fund Expenditures, FY2011	Change in State Federal Fund Expenditures, FY2008 to FY2011
Alabama	$6,291	$9,067	$2,776
Alaska	$2,314	$3,174	$860
Arizona	$7,820	$10,499	$2,679
Arkansas	$4,806	$7,026	$2,220
California	$56,211	$91,459	$35,248
Colorado	$4,739	$8,813	$4,074
Connecticut	$2,117	$2,520	$403
Delaware	$1,113	$1,848	$735
Florida	$18,754	$24,999	$6,245

State	State Federal Funds Expenditures, FY2008	State Federal Fund Expenditures, FY2011	Change in State Federal Fund Expenditures, FY2008 to FY2011
Georgia	$10,268	$14,217	$3,949
Hawaii	$1,760	$2,554	$794
Idaho	$2,005	$3,014	$1,009
Illinois	$11,073	$16,185	$5,112
Indiana	$7,818	$10,596	$2,778
Iowa	$4,565	$6,088	$1,523
Kansas	$3,522	$3,865	$343
Kentucky	$6,720	$9,763	$3,043
Louisiana	$12,883	$12,406	($477)
Maine	$2,182	$3,000	$818
Maryland	$6,561	$10,621	$4,060
Massachusetts	$2,525	$3,739	$1,214
Michigan	$12,660	$22,415	$9,755
Minnesota	$6,264	$9,468	$3,204
Mississippi	$6,434	$9,578	$3,144
Missouri	$5,632	$10,294	$4,662
Montana	$1,646	$2,380	$734
Nebraska	$2,411	$3,220	$809
Nevada	$1,780	$2,642	$862
New Hampshire	$1,498	$1,938	$440
New Jersey	$8,851	$13,518	$4,667
New Mexico	$4,506	$5,716	$1,210
New York	$34,680	$44,707	$10,027
North Carolina	$10,914	$17,605	$6,691
North Dakota	$1,241	$1,801	$560
Ohio	$9,655	$14,431	$4,776
Oklahoma	$9,030	$10,048	$1,018
Oregon	$4,625	$9,334	$4,709
Pennsylvania	$18,037	$29,977	$11,940
Rhode Island	$1,939	$3,085	$1,146
South Carolina	$6,654	$12,844	$6,190
South Dakota	$1,182	$1,671	$489
Tennessee	$9,343	$13,930	$4,587
Texas	$25,023	$35,901	$10,878
Utah	$2,503	$3,954	$1,451

State	State Federal Funds Expenditures, FY2008	State Federal Fund Expenditures, FY2011	Change in State Federal Fund Expenditures, FY2008 to FY2011
Vermont	$1,312	$1,864	$552
Virginia	$6,342	$9,832	$3,490
Washington	$6,678	$8,543	$1,865
West Virginia	$3,287	$4,638	$1,351
Wisconsin	$7,534	$12,236	$4,702
Wyoming	$476	$1,737	$1,261
Total	$388,184	$574,760	$186,576

Source: CRS computations from National Association of State Budget Officers, *State Expenditure Report: FY2009*, Washington, DC, p. 6, at http://nasbo.org/LinkClick.aspx?fileticket=%2bPqnI4oZw2I%3d&tabid=79 and National Association of State Budget Officers, *State Expenditure Report: FY2010*, Washington, DC, December 2011, p. 7, at http://nasbo.org/LinkClick.aspx?fileticket=5VMZ59stp1w%3d&tabid=38.

Notes: FY2011 state federal fund expenditures are estimated from state budget documents.

Other State Funds Expenditures

States increased spending from their other state funds expenditures budgets from FY2008 to FY2011. States spent $376.9 billion from their respective other state funds expenditure budgets in FY2008, $400.1 billion in FY2009, $411.7 billion in FY2010, and an estimated $434.6 billion in FY2011.

As shown in **Table 5**, other state funds expenditures increased $57.7 billion from FY2008 to FY2011, with 12 states decreasing their other state funds expenditures and 38 states increasing their other state funds expenditures.

Table 5. Change in Other State Funds Expenditures, FY2008-FY2011

($ in millions)

State	Other State Funds Expenditures, FY2008	Other State Funds Expenditures, FY2011	Change in Other State Funds Expenditures, FY2008 to FY2011
Alabama	$4,537	$4,910	$373
Alaska	$4,226	$1,643	($2,583)
Arizona	$6,405	$9,654	$3,249
Arkansas	$7,756	$8,782	$1,026
California	$26,674	$31,219	$4,545
Colorado	$12,482	$12,665	$183
Connecticut	$3,494	$3,675	$181
Delaware	$3,811	$3,090	($721)
Florida	$14,916	$20,096	$5,180

State	Other State Funds Expenditures, FY2008	Other State Funds Expenditures, FY2011	Change in Other State Funds Expenditures, FY2008 to FY2011
Georgia	$8,773	$8,326	($447)
Hawaii	$3,376	$3,117	($259)
Idaho	$1,097	$1,621	$524
Illinois	$11,047	$15,296	$4,249
Indiana	$3,380	$3,309	($71)
Iowa	$5,668	$6,534	$866
Kansas	$2,787	$4,824	$2,037
Kentucky	$6,941	$6,978	$37
Louisiana	$5,342	$9,237	$3,895
Maine	$2,053	$2,191	$138
Maryland	$8,520	$9,830	$1,310
Massachusetts	$10,928	$17,719	$6,791
Michigan	$21,081	$19,018	($2,063)
Minnesota	$3,891	$5,289	$1,398
Mississippi	$4,029	$5,589	$1,560
Missouri	$7,165	$6,371	($794)
Montana	$1,810	$2,083	$273
Nebraska	$3,053	$3,260	$207
Nevada	3,028	$2,284	($744)
New Hampshire	$1,680	$2,042	$362
New Jersey	$5,233	$3,694	($1,539)
New Mexico	$3,091	$3,910	$819
New York	$26,122	$31,163	$5,041
North Carolina	$10,098	$14,543	$4,445
North Dakota	$1,125	$1,567	$442
Ohio	$20,633	$17,217	($3,416)
Oklahoma	$4,803	$5,267	$464
Oregon	$10,763	$17,507	$6,744
Pennsylvania	$12,952	$14,409	$1,457
Rhode Island	$1,589	$2,121	$532
South Carolina	$6,866	$7,767	$901
South Dakota	$842	$912	$70
Tennessee	$4,969	$5,554	$585
Texas	$12,634	$16,742	$4,108
Utah	$3,033	$4,662	$1,629

State	Other State Funds Expenditures, FY2008	Other State Funds Expenditures, FY2011	Change in Other State Funds Expenditures, FY2008 to FY2011
Vermont	$2,734	$2,055	($679)
Virginia	$13,040	$14,839	$1,799
Washington	$8,617	$7,037	($1,580)
West Virginia	$11,422	$12,998	$1,576
Wisconsin	$15,028	$17,043	$2,015
Wyoming	$1,350	$2,940	$1,590
Total Change	$376,894	$434,599	$57,705

Source: CRS computations from National Association of State Budget Officers, *State Expenditure Report: FY2009*, Washington, DC, p. 6, at http://nasbo.org/LinkClick.aspx?fileticket=%2bPqnl4oZw2I%3d&tabid=79 and National Association of State Budget Officers, *State Expenditure Report: FY2010*, Washington, DC, December 2011, p. 7, at http://nasbo.org/LinkClick.aspx?fileticket=5VMZ59stp1w%3d&tabid=38.

Notes: FY2011 state other state fund expenditures are estimated from state budget documents.

State Bonds Expenditures

In FY2008, states spent $34.8 billion from their respective state bonds fund expenditure budgets. That amount increased to $35.9 billion in FY2009, $37.9 billion in FY2010, and an estimated $41.5 billion in FY2011. As shown in **Table 6**, eight states (Colorado, Kentucky, Montana, Nebraska, New Mexico, South Carolina, Wisconsin, and Wyoming) had no state bonds fund expenditures in FY2011. The remaining 42 states collectively increased their state bond fund expenditures by almost $6.7 billion from FY2008 to FY2011, with 18 states decreasing their state bonds fund expenditures, 24 states increasing their state bonds fund expenditures, and the remaining 8 states reporting no change in their state bond fund expenditures.

Table 6. Change in State Bonds Fund Expenditures, FY2008-FY2011

($ in millions)

State	State Bonds Fund Expenditures, FY2008	State Bonds Fund Expenditures, FY2011	Change in State Bonds Fund Expenditures, FY2008 to FY2011
Alabama	$552	$359	($193)
Alaska	$26	$228	$202
Arizona	$654	$435	($219)
Arkansas	$63	$83	$20
California	$8,405	$13,195	$4,790
Colorado	$0	$0	$0
Connecticut	$2,032	$2,381	$349
Delaware	$275	$203	($72)
Florida	$3,196	$1,377	($1,819)

State	State Bonds Fund Expenditures, FY2008	State Bonds Fund Expenditures, FY2011	Change in State Bonds Fund Expenditures, FY2008 to FY2011
Georgia	$1,519	$669	($850)
Hawaii	$617	$582	($35)
Idaho	$31	$27	($4)
Illinois	$306	$1,839	$1,533
Indiana	$161	$100	($61)
Iowa	$29	$568	$539
Kansas	$278	$362	$84
Kentucky	$0	$0	$0
Louisiana	$291	$580	$289
Maine	$108	$122	$14
Maryland	$839	$1,082	$243
Massachusetts	$1,420	$1,835	$415
Michigan	$419	$201	($218)
Minnesota	$691	$847	$156
Mississippi	$234	$266	$32
Missouri	$551	$447	($104)
Montana	$0	$0	$0
Nebraska	$0	$0	$0
Nevada	401	$222	($179)
New Hampshire	$114	$133	$19
New Jersey	$1,508	$1,701	$193
New Mexico	$583	$0	($583)
New York	$1,869	$3,582	$1,713
North Carolina	$200	$473	$273
North Dakota	$27	$21	($6)
Ohio	$753	$1,017	$264
Oklahoma	$104	$277	$173
Oregon	$185	$507	$322
Pennsylvania	$738	$561	($177)
Rhode Island	$185	$112	($73)
South Carolina	$118	$0	($118)
South Dakota	$17	$50	$33
Tennessee	$151	$193	$42
Texas	$2,256	$1,259	($997)
Utah	$3	$46	$43

State	State Bonds Fund Expenditures, FY2008	State Bonds Fund Expenditures, FY2011	Change in State Bonds Fund Expenditures, FY2008 to FY2011
Vermont	$37	$86	$49
Virginia	$849	$1,364	$515
Washington	$1,821	$2,025	$204
West Virginia	$177	$63	($114)
Wisconsin	$0	$0	$0
Wyoming	$0	$0	$0
Total Change	$34,793	$41,480	$6,687

Source: CRS computations from National Association of State Budget Officers, *State Expenditure Report: FY2009*, Washington, DC, p. 6, at http://nasbo.org/LinkClick.aspx?fileticket=%2bPqnl4oZw2l%3d&tabid=79 and National Association of State Budget Officers, *State Expenditure Report: FY2010*, Washington, DC, December 2011, p. 7, at http://nasbo.org/LinkClick.aspx?fileticket=5VMZ59stp1w%3d&tabid=38.

Notes: FY2011 state bonds fund expenditures are estimated from state budget documents.

State Capital Expenditures

The total state expenditures amounts presented in **Table 2** included state capital expenditures. As mentioned previously, state capital spending totaled $80.3 billion in FY2008, $84.2 billion in FY2009, $86.1 billion in FY2010, and an estimated $86.1 billion in FY2011.[35] As shown in **Table 7**, five states (Hawaii, Montana, New Mexico, South Carolina, and Wisconsin) reported that they did not make any state capital expenditures in FY2011. The remaining 45 states collectively increased their state capital fund expenditures by more than $5.7 billion from FY2008 to FY2011, with 25 states decreasing their state capital fund expenditures, 23 states increasing their state capital fund expenditures, and the remaining 2 states reporting that they did not change their state capital fund expenditures.

Table 7. Change in State Capital Fund Expenditures, FY2008-FY2011

($ in millions)

State	State Capital Fund Expenditures, FY2008	State Capital Fund Expenditures, FY2011	Change in State Capital Fund Expenditures, FY2008 to FY2011
Alabama	$1,256	$1,291	$35
Alaska	$2,606	$2,345	($261)
Arizona	$1,234	$1,252	$18
Arkansas	$107	$120	$13

---

[35] National Association of State Budget Officers, *State Expenditure Report: Fiscal Year 2009*, Washington, DC, December 2010, p. 80, at http://www.nasbo.org/LinkClick.aspx?fileticket=w7RqO74llEw%3d&tabid=79; and National Association of State Budget Officers, *State Expenditure Report: Fiscal Year 2010*, Washington, DC, December 2011, p. 78, at http://nasbo.org/LinkClick.aspx?fileticket=5VMZ59stp1w%3d&tabid=38.

State	State Capital Fund Expenditures, FY2008	State Capital Fund Expenditures, FY2011	Change in State Capital Fund Expenditures, FY2008 to FY2011
California	$5,210	$8,332	$3,122
Colorado	$1,798	$1,174	($624)
Connecticut	$2,032	$2,381	$349
Delaware	$652	$544	($108)
Florida	$12,671	$9,608	($3,063)
Georgia	$3,229	$1,916	($1,313)
Hawaii	$1,047	$0	($1,047)
Idaho	$479	$657	$178
Illinois	$2,378	$4,571	$2,193
Indiana	$477	$386	($91)
Iowa	$598	$954	$356
Kansas	$782	$1,180	$398
Kentucky	$875	$667	($208)
Louisiana	$1,710	$2,384	$674
Maine	$235	$363	$128
Maryland	$2,980	$1,576	($1,404)
Massachusetts	$1,985	$2,510	$525
Michigan	$1,832	$2,327	$495
Minnesota	$1,503	$2040	$537
Mississippi	$1,384	$1,226	($158)
Missouri	$223	$165	($58)
Montana	$0	$0	$0
Nebraska	$851	$809	($42)
Nevada	1,240	$984	($256)
New Hampshire	$300	$287	($13)
New Jersey	$4,896	$4,695	($201)
New Mexico	$866	$0	($866)
New York	$6,131	$7,845	$1,714
North Carolina	$0	$484	$484
North Dakota	$403	$565	$162
Ohio	$3,004	$3,623	$619
Oklahoma	$1,572	$2,578	$1,006
Oregon	$310	$674	$364
Pennsylvania	$738	$561	($177)
Rhode Island	$429	$318	($111)

State	State Capital Fund Expenditures, FY2008	State Capital Fund Expenditures, FY2011	Change in State Capital Fund Expenditures, FY2008 to FY2011
South Carolina	$436	$0	($436)
South Dakota	$74	$100	$26
Tennessee	$1,609	$1,516	($93)
Texas	$148	$3,307	$3,159
Utah	$1,735	$1,323	($412)
Vermont	$225	$344	$119
Virginia	$1,192	$1,248	$56
Washington	$3,576	$3,321	($255)
West Virginia	$1,091	$1,280	$189
Wisconsin	$0	$0	$0
Wyoming	$239	$225	($14)
Total Change	$80,347	$86,056	$5,709

Source: CRS computations from National Association of State Budget Officers, *State Expenditure Report: FY2009*, Washington, DC, p. 6, at http://nasbo.org/LinkClick.aspx?fileticket=%2bPqnl4oZw2l%3d&tabid=79 and National Association of State Budget Officers, *State Expenditure Report: FY2010*, Washington, DC, December 2011, p. 80, at http://nasbo.org/LinkClick.aspx?fileticket=5VMZ59stp1w%3d&tabid=38.

Notes: FY2011 state capital fund expenditures are estimated from state budget documents.

Federal Assistance and State Fiscal Stress

As the data in the preceding tables indicate, from FY2008 to FY2011, states became more reliant on federal assistance. For example, as mentioned previously, the states' federal funds expenditures increased nearly $186.6 billion from FY2008 to FY2011, compared to an increase of $57.7 billion from the states' other state funds budgets, an increase of $6.7 billion from the states' bonds budgets, and a decrease of nearly $42.7 billion from the states' general fund budgets.

Also, as shown in **Table 8**, the total amount of state federal assistance has increased each fiscal year since FY2000, reaching nearly $574.8 billion in FY2011, more than one-third (34.1%) of total state expenditures. State budget officials anticipate that this upward trend in state federal assistance will end over the next several years as ARRA-related funding is exhausted and federal policymakers scrutinize the federal budget in an effort to address the federal budget deficit. President Obama's FY2012 budget request supports this view, projecting a decline in federal grant-in-aid funding for state and local governments combined from $625.2 billion in FY2011 to $584.3 billion in FY2012 and $567.5 billion in FY2013.[36]

---

[36] U.S. Office of Management and Budget, *Budget of the United States Government, Fiscal Year 2012, Historical Tables*, Washington, DC, 2010, p. 251, at http://www.whitehouse.gov/sites/default/files/omb/budget/fy2012/assets/hist.pdf.

Table 8. Total Amount of State Federal Assistance and Federal Assistance as a Share of Total State Expenditures (Capital Inclusive), FY2000-FY2011

($ in millions)

FY	Total Amount of State Federal Assistance	% Share of Total State Expenditures
2000	$241,317	26.0%
2001	$260,567	25.8%
2002	$295,752	26.9%
2003	$325,102	28.7%
2004	$343,561	29.5%
2005	$365,787	28.9%
2006	$368,668	27.8%
2007	$379,271	26.5%
2008	$388,184	26.3%
2009	$462,980	29.7%
2010	$552,655	34.1%
2011 est.	$574,760	34.1%

Source: National Association of State Budget Officers, *State Expenditure Report [FYs 2000-2009]*, Washington, DC, all pp. 4, 8, at http://www.nasbo.org/Publications/StateExpenditureReport/StateExpenditureReportArchives/ tabid/107/Default.aspx; and National Association of State Budget Officers, *State Expenditure Report: FY2010*, Washington, DC, December 2011, p. 7, at http://nasbo.org/LinkClick.aspx?fileticket=5VMZ59stp1w%3d&tabid= 38.

Consequences for State Policymakers

The states' increased reliance on federal assistance has consequences for both state and federal policymakers. For example, in the past, state political leaders have generally welcomed increased levels of federal assistance while, at the same time, requesting that states be provided maximum feasible flexibility in the use of the grant funds. For example, the National Governors Association (NGA) adopted a permanent policy statement on state-federal relations in 1993, which has been subsequently reaffirmed on several occasions. NGA recommends, among other actions, that the federal government avoid preemption of state laws and policies, preserve state standards, not interfere with state revenue systems, avoid unfunded federal mandates, and provide maximum state flexibility in the use of the federal funds without specific set-asides.[37]

With the notable exception of a few governors who objected to federal conditions attached to ARRA-funded, optional unemployment insurance modernization incentive payments and a few states which refused federal funding related to the implementation of health care reform under P.L. 111-148, the Patient Protection and Affordable Care Act, state policymakers have generally welcomed the recent increase in state federal assistance as a means to help them cope with reductions in state revenues. It is possible, however, that this increased reliance on state federal

---

[37] National Governors Association, "Policy Statement: Permanent Policy. Principles for State-Federal Relations," Washington, DC, at http://www.nga.org/cms/render/live/en/sites/NGA/home/federal-relations/nga-policy-positions/ page-ec-policies/col2-content/main-content-list/title_principles-for-state-federal-relations.html.

assistance might also further limit the states' ability to determine their own policy choices. For example, the need to comply with federal conditions attached to the increased level of federal funds may limit the states' ability to design programs in a way that they believe best meets their needs, which could lead to the federal government substituting its policy preferences for the state's policy preferences. Also, given the current relatively low rate of growth for state tax revenue, the states' increased reliance on federal assistance could limit the states' ability to finance non-federal programs because many federal grants, including Medicaid, have mandatory state matching requirements.

It could also be argued that the states' increased reliance on federal assistance could induce a moral hazard issue by encouraging states to expect similar increases in federal assistance during future economic slowdowns. The concern is that by providing states additional federal assistance the states' "incentives to properly manage risks," by taking such actions as fully funding their "rainy day" reserve funds or making other policy choices to restrain state budget growth during good economic times, could be weakened.[38]

Consequences for Congress

The states' increased reliance on federal assistance could make it more difficult for Congress to make quick and deep reductions in state federal assistance because such actions could lead state governments to take actions, such as laying off public employees, cutting back on state service levels, or increasing state taxes and fees, that could have an adverse effect on the national economic recovery. It could also be argued that many states would have to take such actions because they presently lack the own-source revenue necessary to absorb a significant reduction in state federal assistance.

The counter-argument is that the consequences of reducing state federal assistance to pre-recession levels may force some state governments to make difficult policy choices, but, given the federal government's budget deficit and debt, federal policymakers face similar difficult choices. In addition, it could be argued that the states' increased reliance on federal assistance has created conditions in which state service and benefits levels have become artificially "elevated" to levels that, in the absence of additional federal assistance, would not have been enacted in the first place. As will be discussed in the next section, this last argument involves value judgments concerning the appropriate size and scope of state government.

Variations in State Fiscal Stress

As mentioned previously, although state economic downturns generally occur around the same time as national recessions, the states' responses to national recessions "vary in magnitude, duration, and timing and do not necessarily coincide with dates identified for national recessions."[39] The variation in the states' economic responses to the most recent recession helps to explain the variation found in the states' change in state general fund expenditures from

---

[38] U.S. Government Accountability Office, *State and Local Governments: Knowledge of Past Recessions Can Inform Future Federal Fiscal Assistance*, GAO-11-401, March 31, 2010, p. 30, at http://www.gao.gov/new.items/d11401.pdf.

[39] Ibid., p. 3.

FY2008 to FY2011, with some states increasing their state general fund expenditures and others cutting them.

Consequences for Congress

GAO has recommended that Congress take variations in state fiscal stress into consideration when deciding whether, when, and how to provide federal assistance to state and local governments during and immediately after national economic downturns.[40] Specifically, GAO found that the federal government has provided fiscal assistance to state and local governments in response to three of the six national recessions since 1974, and, after examining the efficacy of those efforts in ameliorating state fiscal stress and enhancing national economic growth, recommended that Congress consider the following when developing a policy strategy to address state and local government fiscal stress during and following national recessions:

- Timing/triggering mechanisms—federal policy strategies specifically intended to stabilize state and local governments' budgets may have to be timed differently than those designed to stimulate the national economy, because state budget difficulties often persist beyond the end of a recession.

- Targeting—if federal fiscal assistance to state and local governments is targeted based on the magnitude of the recession's effect on each state's economy, this approach can facilitate economic recovery and moderate fiscal distress at the state and local level.

- Temporary—while a federal fiscal stimulus strategy can increase economic growth in the short run, such efforts can contribute to the federal budget deficit if allowed to run too long after entering a period of strong recovery.

- Consistency—the design of federal fiscal assistance occurs in tandem with consideration of the impact these strategies can have on other federal policy objectives. For example, a standby federal fiscal assistance policy could induce moral hazard by encouraging state or local governments to expect similar federal action in future crises, thereby weakening their incentives to properly manage risks. Another consideration is the policy objective of maintaining accountability while promoting flexibility in state spending. Past studies have shown that unrestricted federal funds are fungible and can be substituted for state funds, and the uses of such funds can be difficult or impossible to track.[41]

GAO provided Congress a list of recommended economic indicators that could be used to serve as triggering mechanisms to either time or target state federal assistance to respond to the effects of a particular recession, including, among others, employment and unemployment data, hourly earnings, personal income, wages and salaries, and weekly hours worked.[42] GAO excluded indicators of state fiscal stress, such as declines in state tax receipts or state budget gaps, "because they are dependent on state government's policy choices and because state definitions and measurement techniques vary for calculations such as budget gaps."[43]

---

[40] Ibid., p. 28.

[41] Ibid., p. 30.

[42] Ibid., p. 32.

[43] Ibid.

Benchmarks for Measuring Variation in State Fiscal Stress

Although GAO chose not to measure variations in state fiscal assistance, one measure of state fiscal stress that is often used is the difference between the state's current and previous year's general fund budget expenditures. It could be argued that if the state is facing a need to reduce its general fund expenditures from the previous year's level, either in real (inflation adjusted) dollars or in current (nominal) dollars, it is experiencing fiscal stress. Generally speaking, after taking into account factors such as state population differences or differences in the size of the states' general fund budgets, as the amount needed to reduce the state's general fund expenditures increases (typically referred to as the state's budget gap), the state's fiscal stress also increases.

Issues with Using State General Fund Expenditures as a Benchmark

The difference between each state's current and previous year general fund budget expenditures is relatively easy to compute and is often used as an indication of state fiscal stress by various organizations. However, as GAO has noted, there is little guidance available to determine if the state's general fund expenditures for the current, or for the previous year, are "appropriate" baselines to use for measuring state fiscal stress. For example, depending on one's personal values concerning the appropriate size and scope of state government, it could be argued that state expenditures are too high or too low. Also, as mentioned previously, in the absence of an agreement concerning which baselines to use in measuring state fiscal stress, it could be argued that the states' current fiscal stress has as much to do with their previous budgetary decisions (or non-decisions) as with the national economic slowdown's adverse effect on state revenue growth. This is an important issue for federal policymakers because if state fiscal stress is viewed as being largely a result of state policy decisions, it is likely that there will be less support for federal action to ease that fiscal stress than would be the case otherwise.

Measuring the Relative Size of State Governments

The data presented in **Table 9** are provided to help inform congressional debate concerning the extent to which the states' varying levels of fiscal stress are due to changing economic conditions or to state policy choices. The data provide a framework for measuring differences in the size of state governments relative to each other, rather than to a preconceived "ideal" state budget that would, by necessity, be based largely on personal value judgments concerning the appropriate size and scope of state government. This information may prove useful as a reference when debating the role of state policy choice in state fiscal stress.

As shown in the table, total state expenditures, both per capita and as a percentage of state GDP, vary.[44]

---

[44] Another factor that could be used to compare total state expenditures is the extent to which the state relies on local governments to provide services. It could be argued that some states look "bigger" than others because they carry greater responsibility for providing services than their local governments when compared to other states. Unfortunately, data on local government finance are typically delayed for at least two years. For example, at the time of this writing, the latest available data at the Bureau of the Census for both state and local government expenditures are for FY2009. Those data indicate that in FY2009 the state share of total state and local government expenditures varied among the states, ranging from 42.5% in Florida to 77.1% in Hawaii. The states' average share of state and local government expenditures was 57.5%, with 27 states below the national average and 23 states above the national average. CRS calculations from U.S. Bureau of the Census, "State and Local Government Finance: 2009 State and Local (continued...)

Table 9. Total State Expenditures, Per Capita FY2011 and Percentage of State GDP FY2010

State	Total State Expenditures FY2011 ($ in millions)	Total State Expenditures FY2011, Per Capita	State GDP FY2010 ($ in millions)	Total State Expenditures FY2010, % of State GDP
Alabama	$20,843	$4,340	$172,567	12.08%
Alaska	$13,923	$19,297	$49,120	28.34%
Arizona	$29,264	$4,563	$253,609	11.54%
Arkansas	$20,333	$6,949	$102,566	19.82%
California	$227,353	$6,088	$1,901,088	11.96%
Colorado	$28,462	$5,642	$257,641	11.05%
Connecticut	$20,545	$5,736	$237,261	8.66%
Delaware	$8,412	$9,338	$62,280	13.51%
Florida	$70,518	$3,731	$747,735	9.43%
Georgia	$39,166	$4,026	$403,070	9.72%
Hawaii	$11,222	$8,210	$66,760	16.81%
Idaho	$7,050	$4,480	$55,435	12.72%
Illinois	$56,222	$4,370	$651,518	8.63%
Indiana	$27,042	$4,159	$275,676	9.81%
Iowa	$18,538	$6,070	$142,698	12.99%
Kansas	$14,778	$5,160	$127,170	11.62%
Kentucky	$25,528	$5,868	$163,269	15.64%
Louisiana	$30,174	$6,626	$218,853	13.79%
Maine	$8,171	$6,129	$51,643	15.82%
Maryland	$34,795	$6,010	$295,304	11.78%
Massachusetts	$51,761	$7,891	$378,729	13.67%
Michigan	$50,020	$5,047	$384,171	13.02%
Minnesota	$32,082	$6,036	$270,039	11.88%
Mississippi	$19,777	$6,640	$97,461	20.29%
Missouri	$24,728	$4,113	$244,016	10.13%
Montana	$6,164	$6,199	$36,067	17.09%
Nebraska	$9,802	$5,351	$89,786	10.92%
Nevada	$8,549	$3,155	$125,650	6.80%
New Hampshire	$5,435	$4,113	$60,283	9.02%
New Jersey	$48,235	$5,477	$487,335	9.90%

(...continued)

Government," Washington, DC, at http://www.census.gov/govs/estimate/.

State	Total State Expenditures FY2011 ($ in millions)	Total State Expenditures FY2011, Per Capita	State GDP FY2010 ($ in millions)	Total State Expenditures FY2010, % of State GDP
New Mexico	$14,829	$7,173	$79,678	18.61%
New York	$132,765	$6,836	$1,159,540	11.45%
North Carolina	$51,124	$5,344	$424,935	12.03%
North Dakota	$4,974	$7,359	$34,685	14.34%
Ohio	$60,314	$5,214	$477,699	12.63%
Oklahoma	$22,067	$5,861	$147,543	14.96%
Oregon	$33,455	$8,693	$174,151	19.21%
Pennsylvania	$70,089	$5,504	$569,679	12.30%
Rhode Island	$8,292	$7,858	$49,234	16.84%
South Carolina	$25,691	$5,530	$164,445	15.62%
South Dakota	$3,781	$4,612	$39,893	9.48%
Tennessee	$30,904	$4,847	$254,806	12.13%
Texas	$94,443	$3,738	$1,207,494	7.82%
Utah	$13,372	$4,826	$114,538	11.67%
Vermont	$4,827	$7,658	$25,620	18.84%
Virginia	$42,470	$5,284	$423,860	10.02%
Washington	$32,430	$4,802	$340,460	9.53%
West Virginia	$21,492	$11,556	$64,642	33.25%
Wisconsin	$42,844	$7,519	$248,265	17.26%
Wyoming	$8,041	$14,149	$38,527	20.87%
Total	$1,687,096	NA	$14,448,494	NA
National Average	$33,742	$5,457	$288,970	11.68%

Source: CRS computations from U.S. Bureau of the Census, "Apportionment Population and Number of Representatives, by State: 2010 Census," December 21, 2010, at http://www.thegreenpapers.com/Census10/; U.S. Department of Commerce, Bureau of Economic Analysis, "Gross Domestic Product By State," Washington, DC, September 29, 2011, at http://www.bea.gov/regional/gsp/default.cfm#download; and National Association of State Budget Officers, *State Expenditure Report: FY2010*, Washington, DC, December 2011, p. 7, at http://nasbo.org/LinkClick.aspx?fileticket=5VMZ59stp1w%3d&tabid=38.

Notes: FY2011 total state expenditures are estimated from state budget documents. The national median for total state expenditures in FY2011, per capita, was $5,642. The national median for total state expenditures in FY2010, as a percentage of state GDP, was 12.13%.

As shown in **Table 9**, in FY2011, total state expenditures ranged from $3,781 million in South Dakota to $227,353 million in California. The national average for total state expenditures was $33,742 million, with 35 states having total state expenditures below the national average and 15 states having total state expenditures above the national average.

In FY2011, total state expenditures on a per capita basis varied from $3,155 in Nevada to $19,297 in Alaska. The national average for total state expenditures on a per capita basis was $4,340, with

21 states having total state expenditures on a per capita below the national average and 29 states having total state expenditures on a per capita basis above the national average.

In FY2010 (the latest data available), state gross domestic product and total state expenditures as a percentage of state gross domestic product varied from state-to-state. State gross domestic product ranged from $25,620 million in Vermont to $1,901,088 million in California. The national average for state gross domestic product was $288,970 million, with 35 states having state gross domestic product below the national average and 15 states having state gross domestic product above the national average.

In FY2010, total state expenditures as a percentage of state gross domestic product ranged from 6.80% in Nevada to 33.25% in West Virginia. The national average for total state expenditures as a percentage of state gross domestic product was 11.68%, with 19 states having total state expenditures as a percentage of state gross domestic product below the national average and 31 states having total state expenditures as a percentage of state gross domestic product above the national average.

Concluding Observations

State policymakers throughout the nation will face at least four significant fiscal challenges in the coming years. First, state budget officials expect relatively low levels of tax revenue growth. If these state revenue estimates prove to be accurate, unless there is growth in other state revenue sources, many states are going to face funding gaps in their general fund budgets for several more years which, given state balanced operating budget requirements, would need to be addressed.[45] Second, ARRA funding, the primary source of state revenue relief over the past two years, is expiring. Third, state federal assistance outside of ARRA is expected to decline, and federal grants to state and local governments are included in federal domestic discretionary spending, an area of the federal budget expected to receive much attention over the next several years by federal policymakers as they seek ways to address the federal deficit and debt. Fourth, projected state costs for Medicaid, state employee pension and retirement health care obligations, and delayed infrastructure projects are also expected to provide continuing budgetary challenges for states.

Given these fiscal challenges, it is likely that states will continue to look to the federal government for financial assistance. Federal assistance could be provided in several ways, for example (1) granting of waivers of federal grant program requirements, (2) temporary or permanent relief from federal grant matching requirements, (3) relaxation or elimination of state program-related maintenance of effort requirements that are often attached to federal grant programs, and (4) providing additional direct federal assistance.

GAO has recommended that Congress consider variations in state fiscal stress when deciding whether, when, and how to provide federal assistance to state and local governments during and immediately after national economic downturns. As mentioned previously, GAO also provided a

---

[45] For further information and analysis of state revenue estimates see Susan K. Urahn and Thomas Gais, "States' Revenue Estimating: Cracks in the Crystal Ball," The Nelson Rockefeller Institute of Government and the Pew Center on the States, Washington, DC, at http://www.pewcenteronthestates.org/uploadedFiles/ States_Revenue_Estimating_final.pdf.

list of economic indicators, such as employment and unemployment data, hourly earnings, personal income, wages and salaries, and weekly hours worked, that could be used as triggers for providing states federal assistance.[46] GAO excluded indicators of state fiscal stress, such as declines in state tax receipts or state budget gaps, "because they are dependent on state government's policy choices and because state definitions and measurement techniques vary for calculations such as budget gaps."[47]

Disagreement over the appropriate size of state government has always been an issue in discussions of the role of federal assistance in state budgeting. The data presented in **Table 9** suggest that state governments, both in terms of total state expenditures on a per capita basis and as a percentage of state GDP, vary in size. Some argue against providing additional federal assistance to states because, in their view, the states' current level of fiscal stress, especially in states with a relatively high level of state expenditures, could have been ameliorated if the states had been more prudent with their fiscal choices prior to the recent recession. Others suggest that the federal government's fiscal challenges have reached a point at which providing additional federal assistance to states is out of the question. Still others assert that if the federal government does not continue to provide the states additional assistance, then the states will take actions that will have an adverse effect on the national economic recovery. Some also contend that the recent increase in federal assistance to states is approaching levels that may lead to a fundamental change in the nature of American federalism. They are concerned that the need to match federal grant money and the increased reliance on federal assistance to provide services could displace state priorities with federal priorities. The data and analysis in this report provide a framework for assisting Congress as it considers these various viewpoints concerning whether, when, and how to provide federal assistance to state and local governments during times of state fiscal stress.

Author Contact Information

Robert Jay Dilger
Senior Specialist in American National Government
rdilger@crs.loc.gov, 7-3110

---

[46] Ibid., p. 32.

[47] Ibid.